This Book Belongs To:

_____

Dealership Owner

As a Dealership Owner, I will thrive to create experiences, build trust, and deliver dreams on wheels, fostering a community.

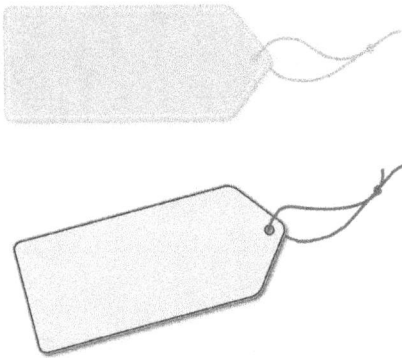

Famous Artist

As a Famous Artist, I will leave strokes of inspiration that transcend the boundaries of time.

Photographer

As a Photographer, I can capture moments, freezing time, revealing the beauty and emotion of every story.

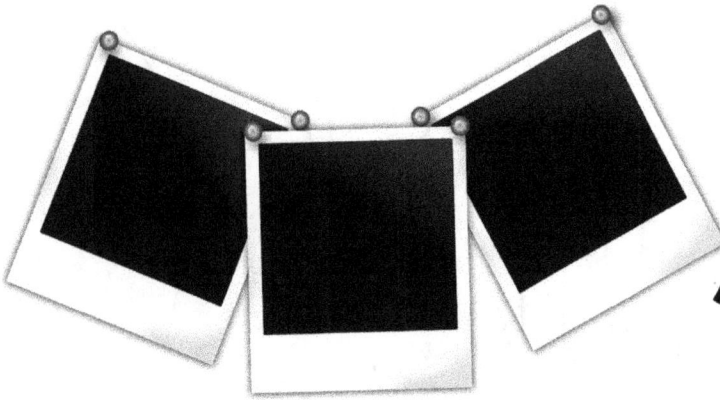

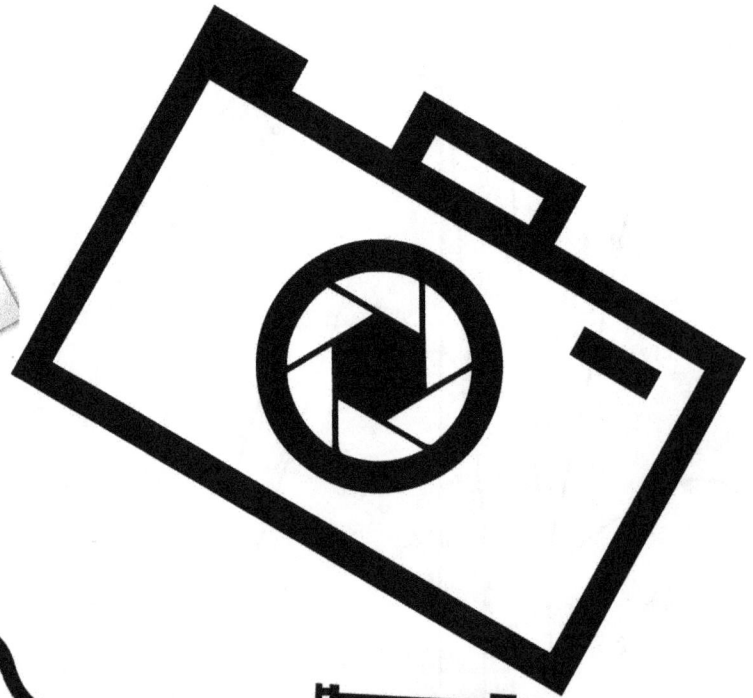

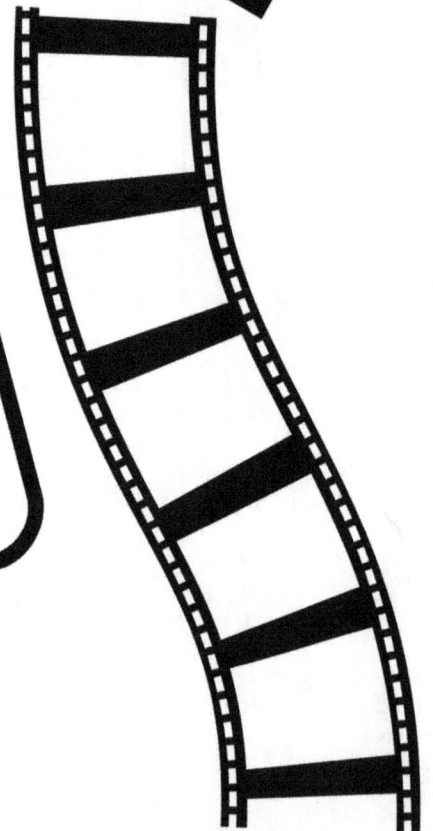

Professional Athlete

As a Professional Athlete, I will work toward triumph, embodying the spirit of determination and victory.

Travel Agent

As a Travel Agent, I will guide journeys of discovery, turning moments into lifelong memories.

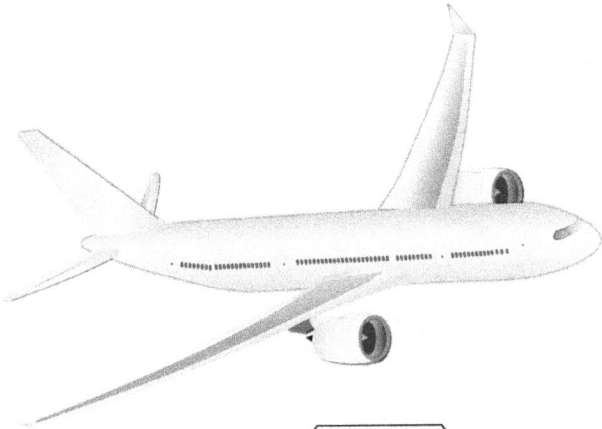

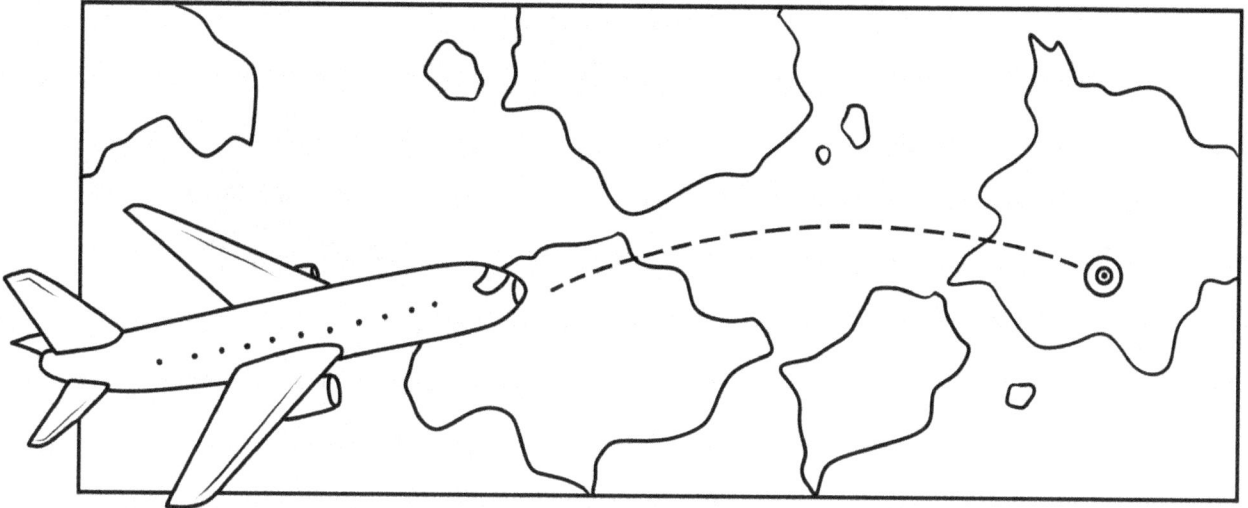

Therapist

As a Therapist, I can listen with a heart full of empathy, offering support and healing to those in need.

Veterinarian

As a Veterinarian, I can heal with compassion, ensuring every paw and wing receives tender care.

Certified Public Accountant

As an Certified Public Accountant, in the knowledge of numbers, I can provide financial empowerment.

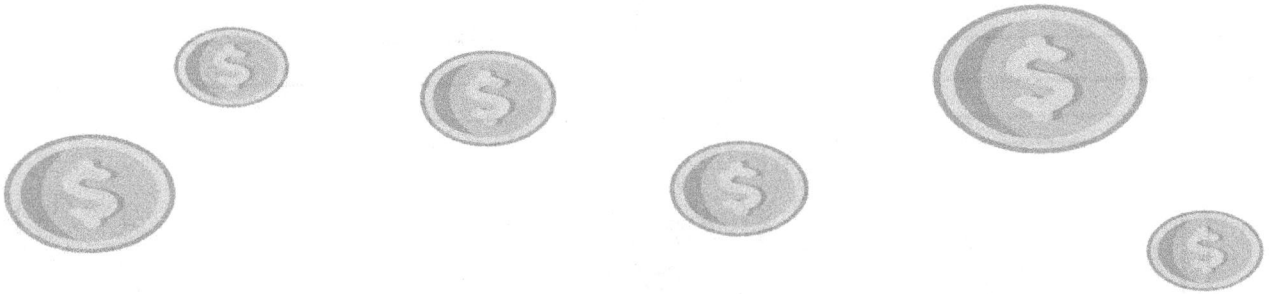

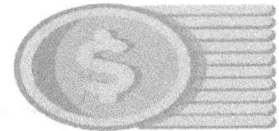

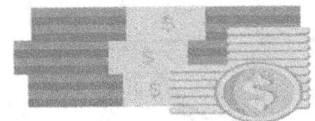

Lawyer

As a Lawyer, I can enforce the means of justice, fighting for equality and fairness in the courtroom.

Principal

As a Principal, I can guide young minds with compassion, and build a foundation for dreams to flourish.

Famous Author

As a Famous Author, I can ignite imaginations, developing words into worlds of fantasy and mystery.

Carpenter

As a Carpenter, I can shape dreams into reality, constructing a masterpiece with my imagination and hands.

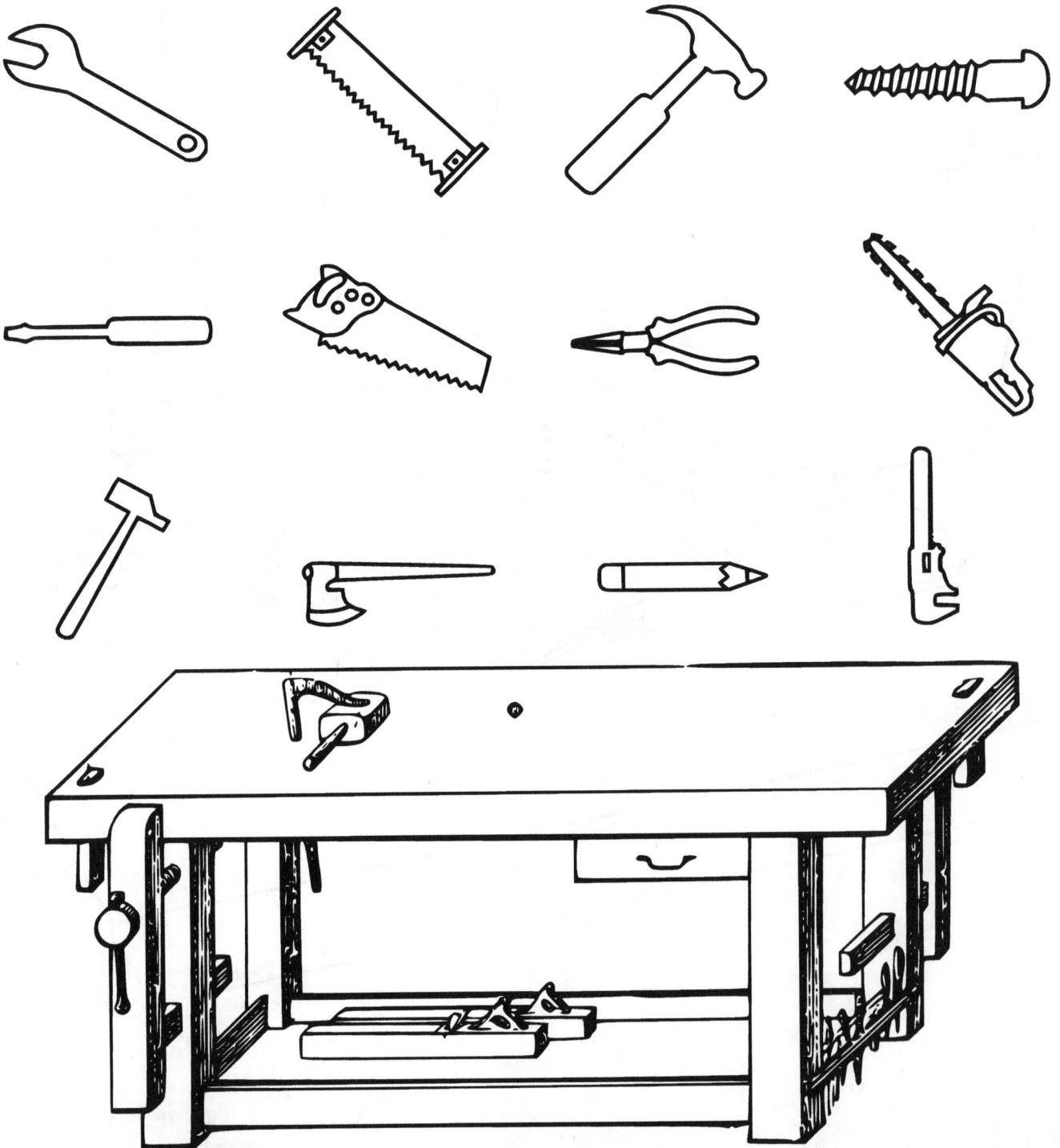

Farmer

As a Farmer, I can sow seeds of joy, nurturing a harvest that sustains both land and spirit.

College Professor

As a College Professor, I can spark the flames of knowledge, lighting the path to infinite possibilities.

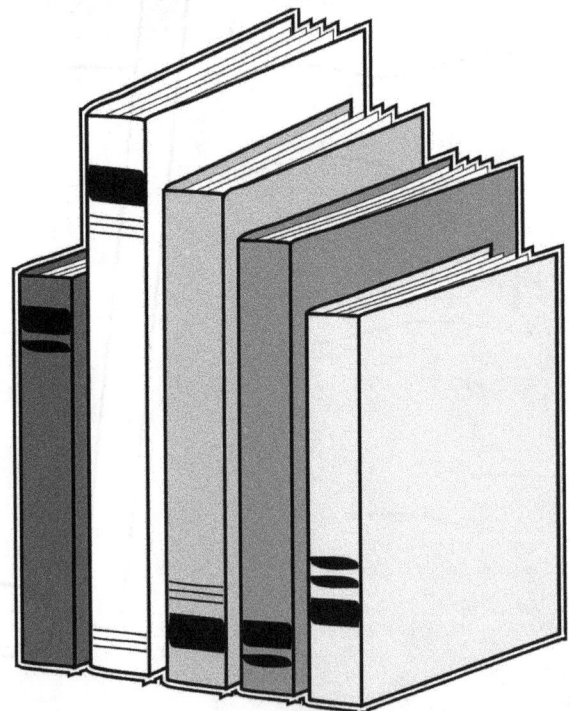

Famous Director

As a Famous Director, I can create dreams on the big screen, turning scripts into cinematic work of art.

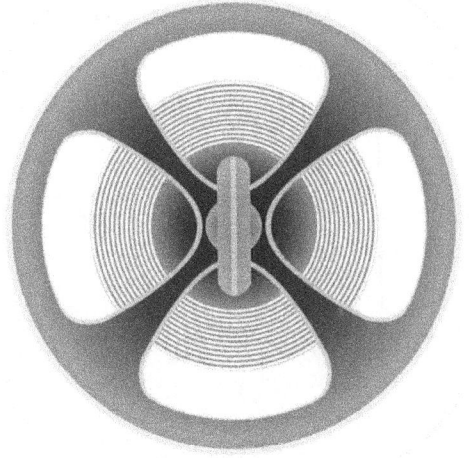

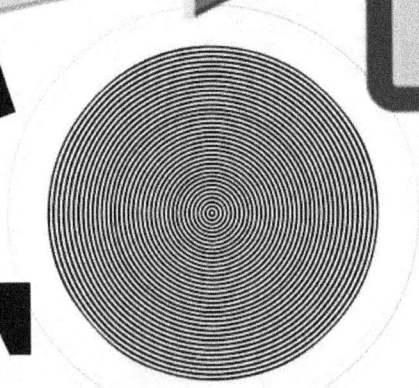

PRODUCTION

SCENE | TAKE

DIRECTOR

CAMERA

DATE

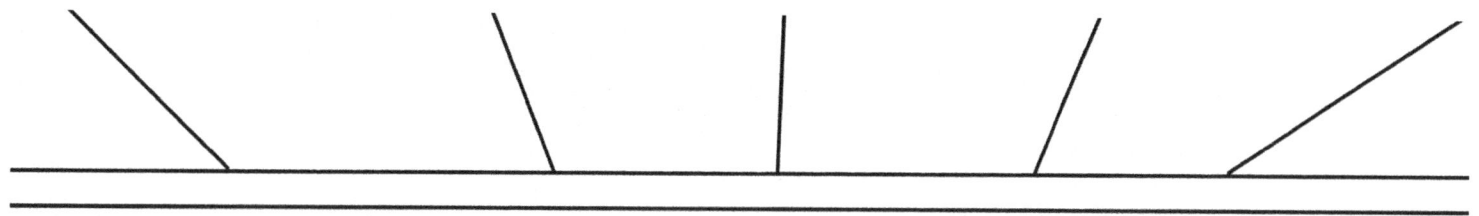

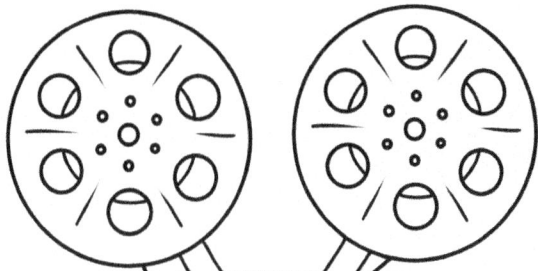

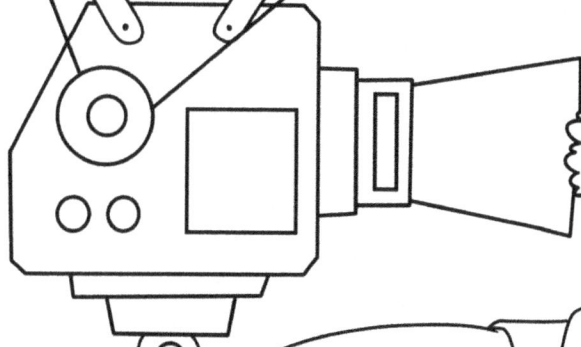

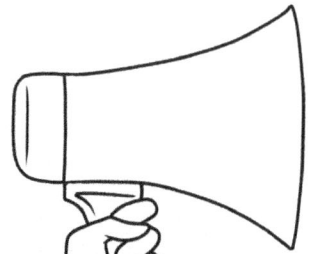

Architect

As an Architect, I can shape dreams into structures, crafting a skyline of boundless aspirations.

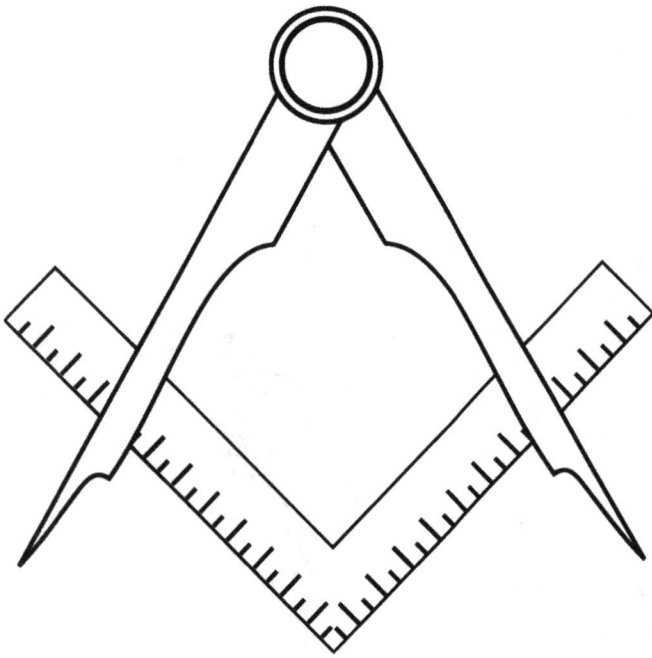

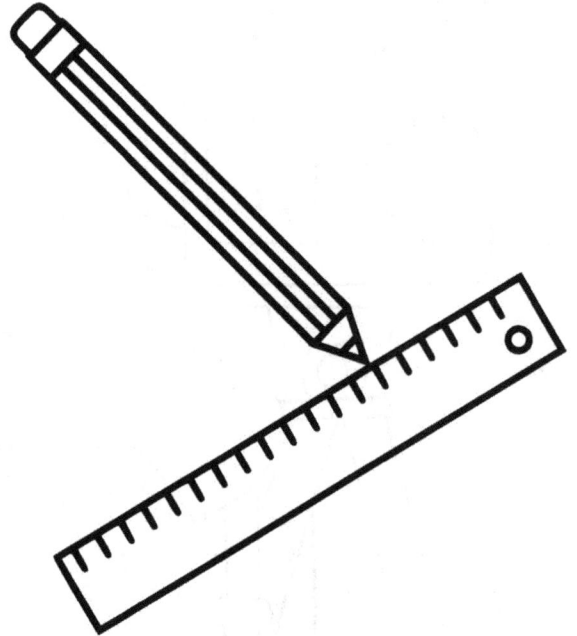

Real Estate Agent

As a Real Estate Agent, I can help turn dreams into reality, unlocking doors to homes to fill with love and joy.

Aerospace Engineer

As a Aerospace Engineer, I will design the wings of human ambition, pushing the boundaries of flight to unlock new horizons and shape the future of exploration.

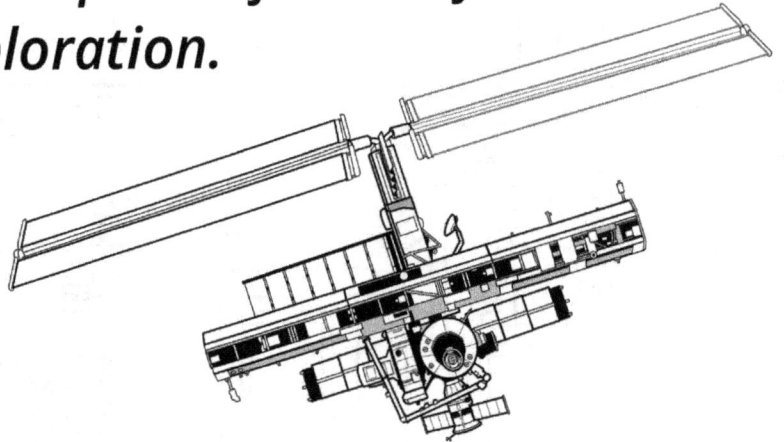

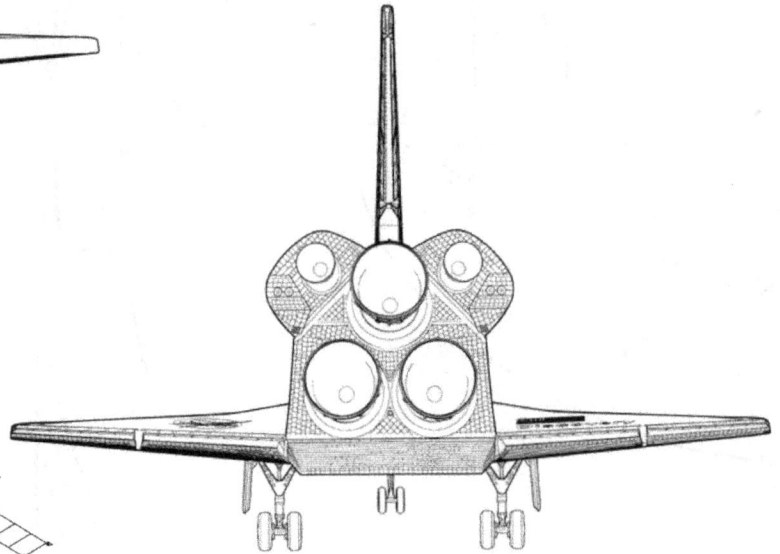

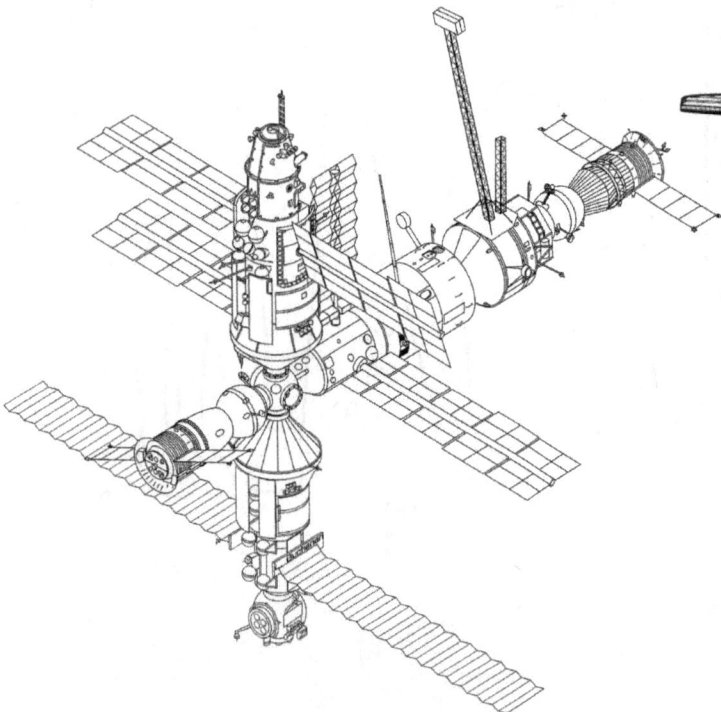

Police Officer

As a Police Officer, I will wear my badge with honor by patrolling with integrity to ensure safety for all.

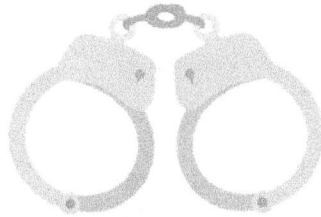

Fire Fighter

As a Firefighter, I can battle flames with bravery, extinguishing fires to protect and save others.

Celebrity Saxophonist

As a Celebrity Saxophone, I can entertain, harmonizing with melodies that soothe the soul.

Private Investigator

As a Private Investigator, I will navigate the shadows of secrecy with tenacity and insight, uncovering truths that lie dormant and delivering justice to those whose stories deserve to be heard.

Dentist

As a Dentist, I can brighten smiles, instilling confidence with every sparkling tooth.

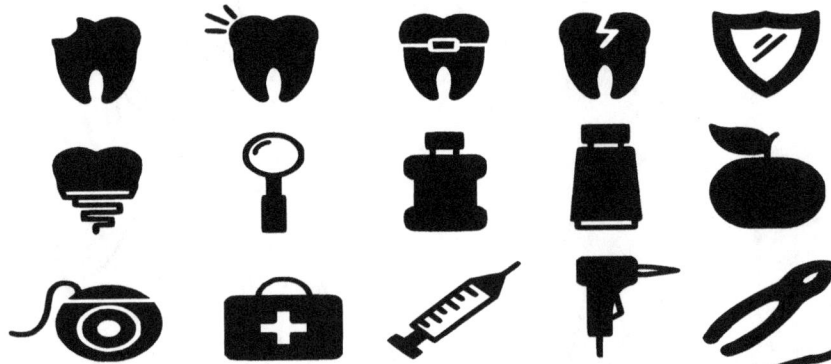

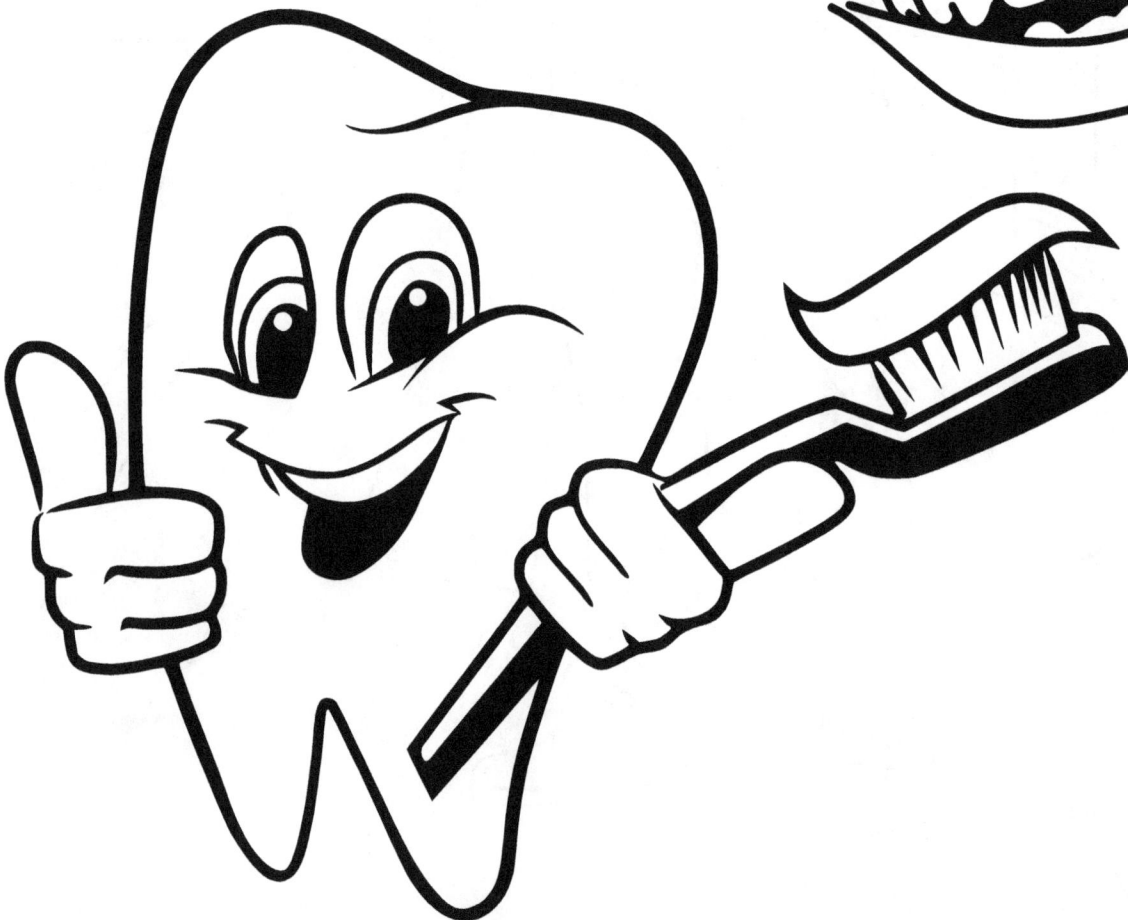

Pilot

As a Pilot, I can soar through the skies, navigating a world and creating priceless memories.

Celebrity Chef

As a Celebrity Chef, I can transform ingredients into art, creating a symphony of flavors that harmonize with the soul.

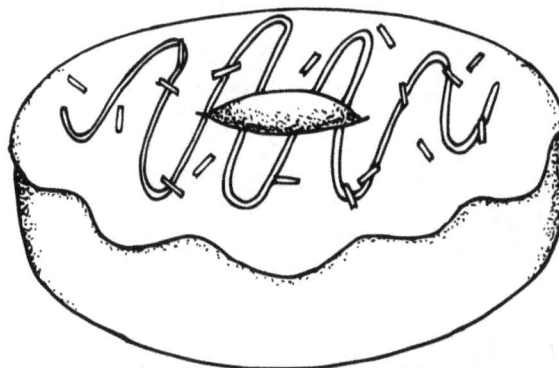

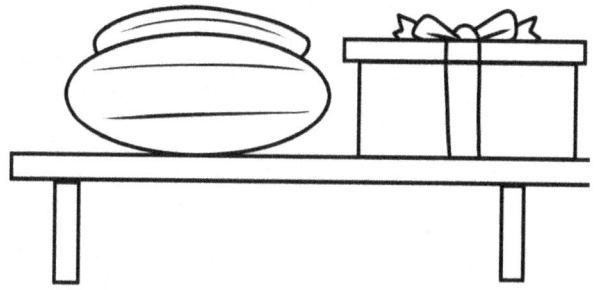

Top News Anchor

As a Top News Anchor, I can unveil stories that are reliable, resonating with the power of awareness.

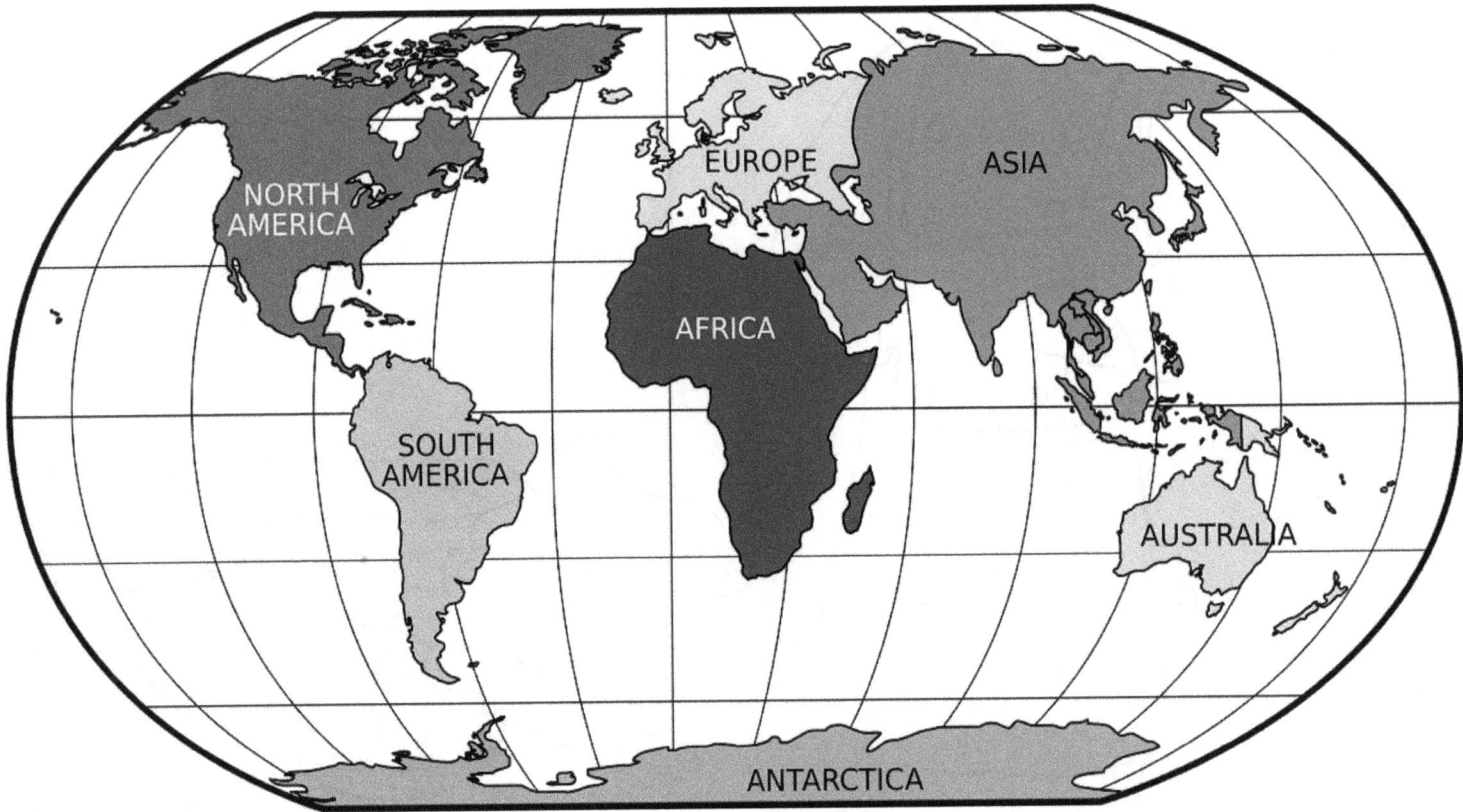

Astronaut

As a Astronaut, I can orbit the stars as I explore the cosmos, reaching for undiscovered realm.

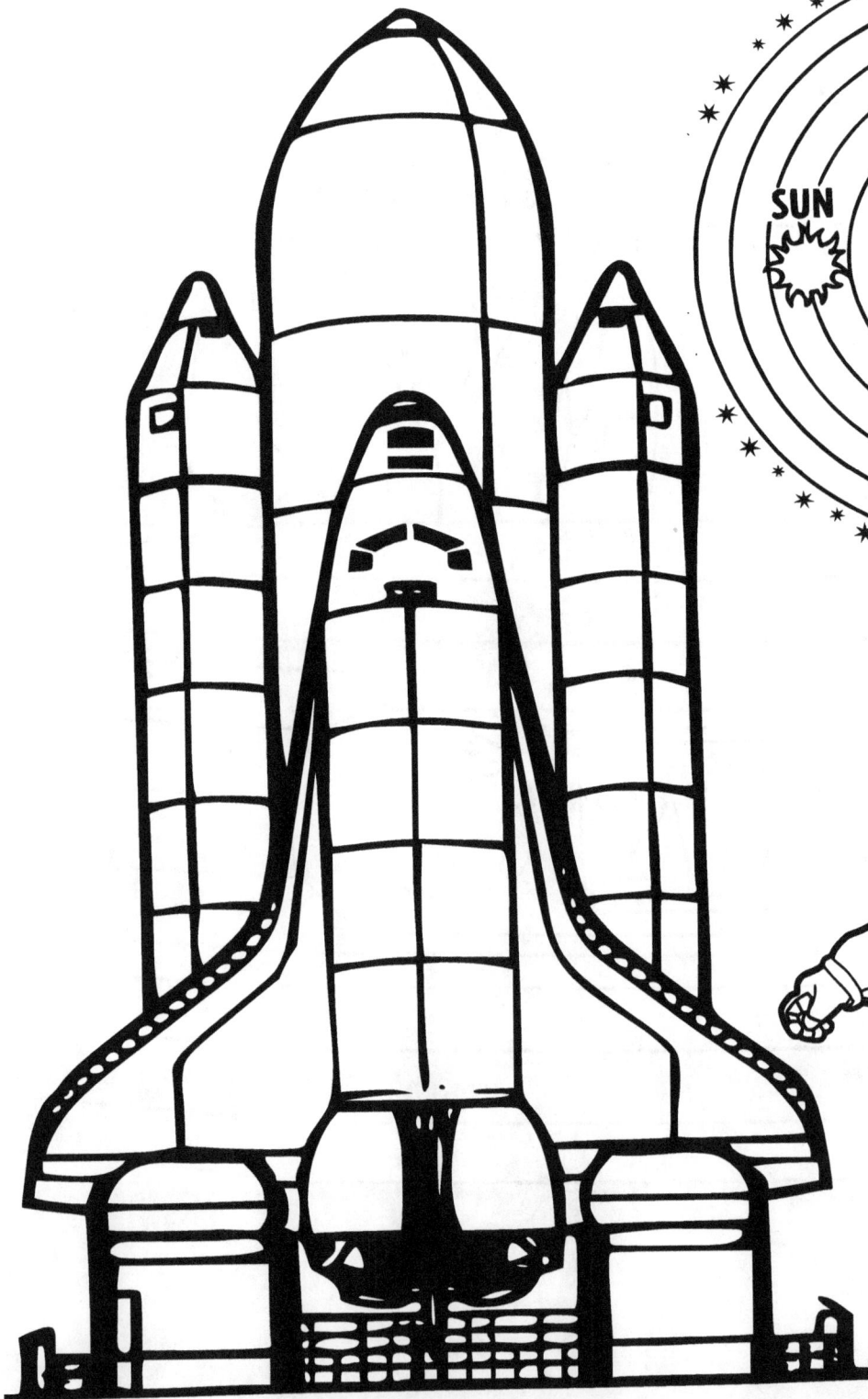

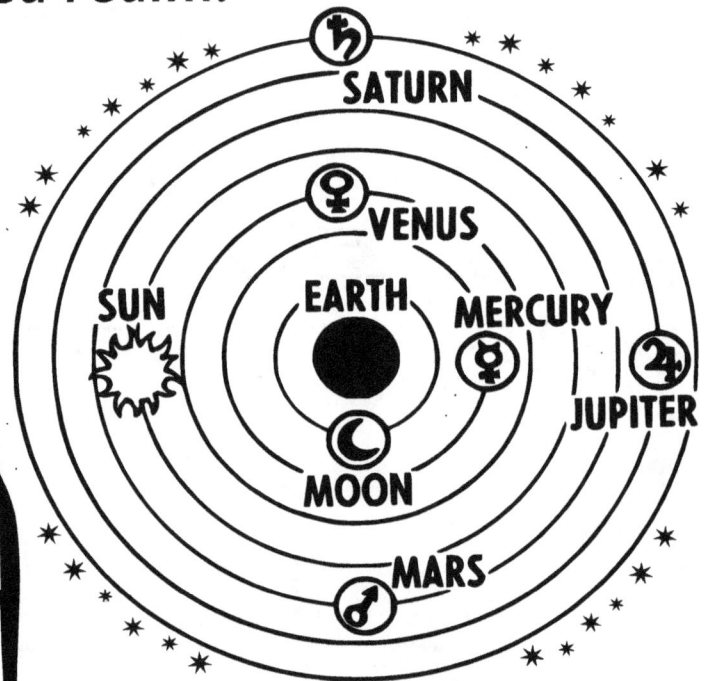

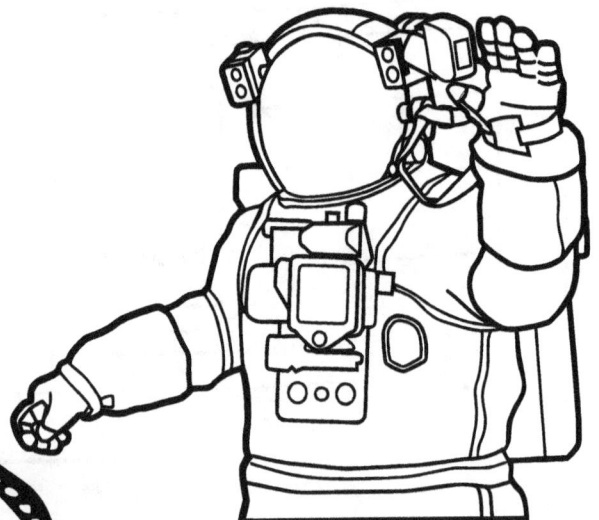

Doctor

As a Doctor, I would demonstrate compassionate for each patient. Leading patients on a journey toward wellness and hope.

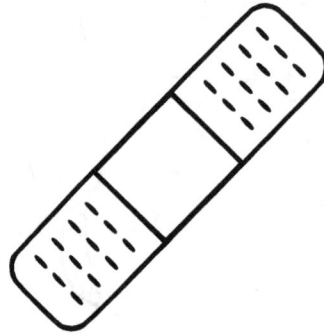

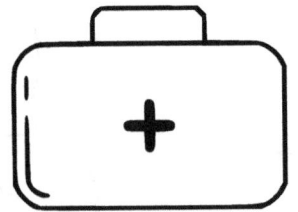

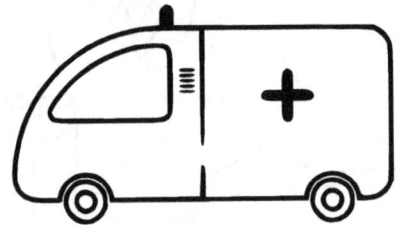

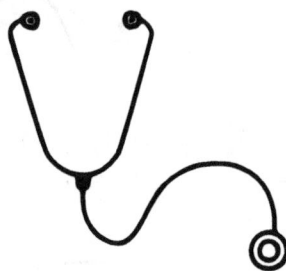

Supreme Court Judge

As a Supreme Court Judge, I can balance the scales of justice, ensuring fairness and equality for all.

JUDGE

President of the United States

As President of the United States , I would lead with wisdom and compassion, shaping the nation where dreams have no limitations. Upholding the terms of democracy with respects to human rights and fundamental freedoms.

Career Word Search

```
X S E R O R E Y A L P E N O H P O X A S A Y R E
Q H Z E N X N Q T Z W I D F S O X Q O S H M E G
W B G T G A O C D E N T I S T L S H R U X K B T
Q R X N S C L O Q M S Z U H P K H O I P W C D D
C Y S E F T Q U F U O R P B W T T B X R R P K L
M W P P G O T T P T V H K Z B C H R V E O P K D
I E O R J R E H P A R G O T O H P B R M T Z Q A
R J I A O A M L W Q Q P C D Q V Z H T E C S E E
I D S C Y F Z V E T E R I N A R I A N C E Q M L
T E C O L L E G E P R O F E S S O R E O R X D W
V Q L H A I R S T Y L I S T L I A O G U I Z E S
X A A R E N G I S E D N O I H S A F A R D K S J
V V P R O F E S S I O N A L A T H L E T E Y F G
R D I O E K N U T F O N J T L F C V T J I W O F
Y Q C H P E V N L T Y N T T W A W C A U V A O A
P K N T P R N U V N A T A S D F W D T D O H G R
H J I U K X J I Q A N S O L I P M Y S G M R Q M
V S R A F J T L G T V K T N C P X B E E N I L E
M E P S N E W S A N C H O R H H A K L R R E H R
M O H U H A O G W U E H D N O Z E R A P D B D V
F E X O Z R A M D O A O Z A P N Z F E T Z E V Z
T F H M E C L B T C E T I H C R A Q R H V R N F
M R R A C C B V R C H S A B L H G U G I T L T E
I O E F D Z V N V A V N G B N Q P R T Z N Y K O
```

ACTOR
FARMER
ASTRONAUT
THERAPIST
HAIRSTYLIST
PHOTOGRAPHER
FASHION DESIGNER
COLLEGE PROFESSOR
PROFESSIONAL ATHLETE

DOCTOR
DENTIST
ARCHITECT
ACCOUNTANT
NEWS ANCHOR
FAMOUS AUTHOR
SAXOPHONE PLAYER
PROFESSIONAL CHEF

LAWYER
PRINCIPAL
CARPENTER
BIOENGINEER
VETERINARIAN
MOVIE DIRECTOR
REAL ESTATE AGENT
SUPREME COURT JUDGE

Career Word Search

```
N W E E C A D G H O D J W J F S O P A G P C K W
K E Y F S T J Q J C R D L M Y K W Q U L A O N Y
W E B D E V E L O P E R X N A V L I S C I E R B
M L G H U J V I T I L L U S T R A T O R N T R V
B H W A R I Q D A S N G S X E O D M F K T S P P
L O L J I O I F G J I O M I E W P O T C E Y P G
S T Z F R T T E F Y E T D G H U E Q W P R L V R
A R S P S B E S U B K C N W T L L R A M O A F A
F R C I U T R R E N G I S E D R O I R E T N I P
P L T H H Y N M L V F R R K I F X C E B C A X H
H R I T P Y S R M F N P B M Y C A D E A E S T I
A U P G P Y Z F N C R I P K Q S S W N M P S S C
R H N K H C H I R O P R A C T O R I G O S E I D
M A R K E T I N G M A N A G E R G U I A N N L E
A A H U Z K A R Y N A I R A R B I L N P I I A S
C M O T I V A T I O N A L S P E A K E R D S N I
I J P Z J M N I T M C H E M I S T T E Y O U R G
S W S S M C Y U R E U R U E D E T B R C O B U N
T W R E U G L R R C N D P O T Y A U G E F A O E
V Y R A T I L I M S P D I P C C H Z U W C S J R
B A Z I A Y T I H R E G A N A M S E L A S S O S
O P T O M E T R I S T O Q N J N F J A Y O R C C
R U J S V H L B V W A M S H T R H F B R H Z H O
K M L A N D S C A P E R O S H F W P R G R I K B
```

NURSE	ARTIST	PAINTER
CHEMIST	INVESTOR	MILITARY
SCIENTIST	LIBRARIAN	JOURNALIST
LANDSCAPER	PHARMACIST	ILLUSTRATOR
OPTOMETRIST	CHIROPRACTOR	SALES MANAGER
WEB DEVELOPER	FOOD INSPECTOR	BUSINESS ANALYST
GRAPHIC DESIGNER	FLIGHT ATTENDANT	MARKETING MANAGER
SOFTWARE ENGINEER	INTERIOR DESIGNER	COMPUTER PROGRAMMER
MOTIVATIONAL SPEAKER		

Find your Career

Find your Career

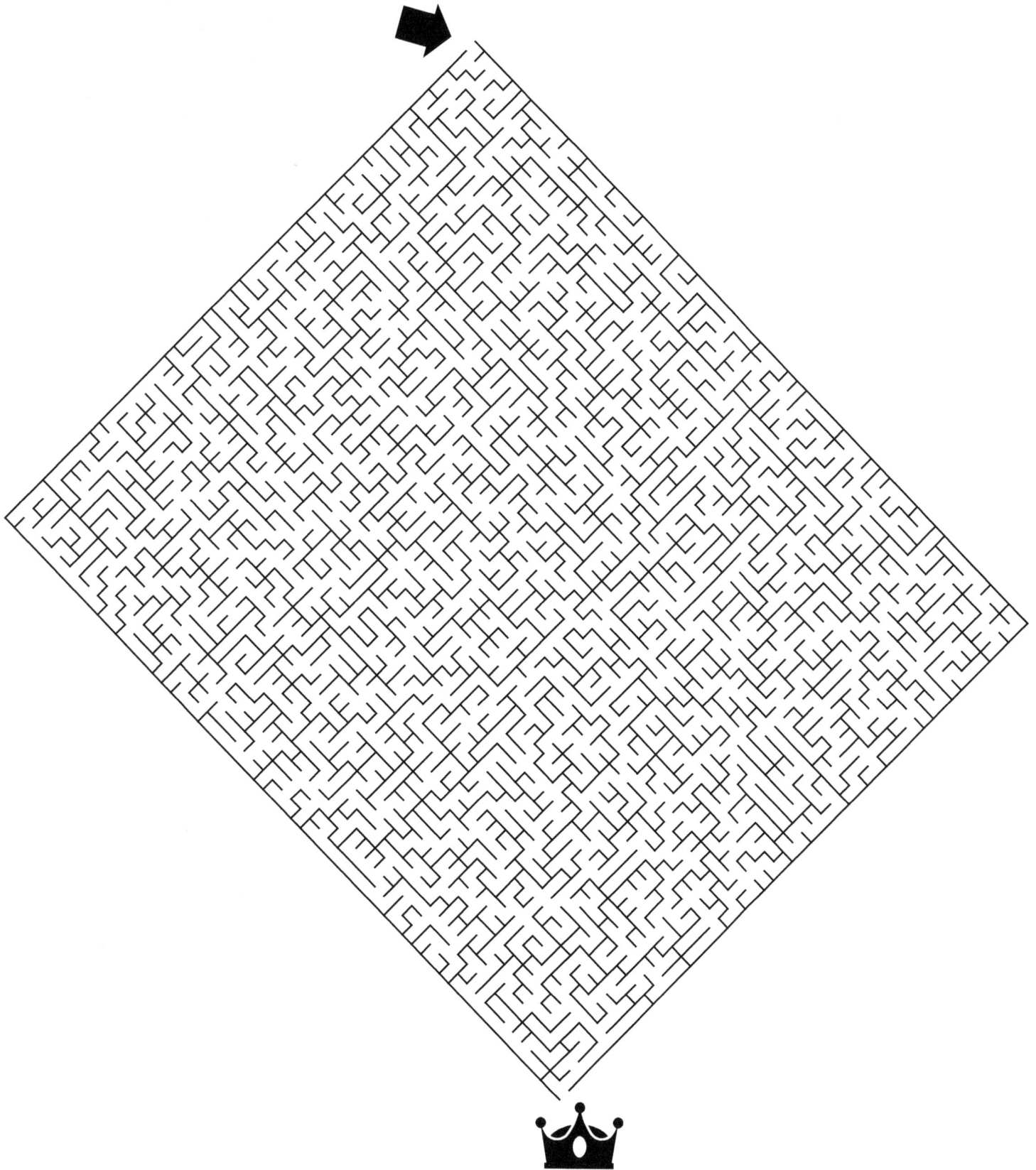

Career Word Search answer

Grid 1

```
X S E R O R E Y A L P E N O H P O X A S A Y R E
Q H Z E N X N Q T Z W I D F S O X Q O S H M E G
W B G T G A O C D E N T I S T L S H R U X K B T
Q R X N S C L O Q M S Z U H P K H O I P W C D D
C Y S E F T Q U F O R P B W T T B X R R P K L
M W P P G O T T P T V H K Z B C H R V E O P K D
I E O R J R E H P A R G O T O H P B R M T Z Q A
R J I A O A M L W Q Q P C D Q V Z H T E C S E E
I D S C Y F Z V E T E R I N A R I A N C E Q M L
T E C O L L E G E P R O F E S S O R E O R X D W
V Q L H A I R S T Y L I S T L I A O G U I Z E S
X A A R E N G I S E D N O I H S A F A R D K S J
V V P R O F E S S I O N A L A T H L E T E Y F G
R D I O E K N U T F O N J T L F C V T J I W O F
Y Q C H P E V N L T Y N T T W A W C A U V A O A
P K N T P R N U V N A T A S D F W D T D O H G R
H J I U K X J I Q A N S O L I P M Y S G M R Q M
V S R A F J T L G T V T V C P X B E E N I L E
M E P S N E W S A N C H O R H H A K L R E H R
M O H U H A O G W U E H D N O Z E R A P D B D V
F E X O Z R A M D O A O Z A P N Z F E T Z E V Z
T F H M E C L B T C E T I H C R A Q R H V R N F
M R R A C C B V R C H S A B L H G U G I T L T E
I O E F D Z V N V A V N G B N Q N P R T Z N Y K O
```

Word List
ACTOR
FARMER
ASTRONAUT
THERAPIST
HAIRSTYLIST
PHOTOGRAPHER
FASHION DESIGNER
COLLEGE PROFESSOR
PROFESSIONAL ATHLETE

DOCTOR
DENTIST
ARCHITECT
ACCOUNTANT
NEWS ANCHOR
FAMOUS AUTHOR
SAXOPHONE PLAYER
PROFESSIONAL CHEF

LAWYER
PRINCIPAL
CARPENTER
BIOENGINEER
VETERINARIAN
MOVIE DIRECTOR
REAL ESTATE AGENT
SUPREME COURT JUDGE

Grid 2

```
N W E E C A D G H O D J W J F S O P A G P C K W
K E Y F S T J Q J C R D L M Y K W Q U L A O N Y
W E B D E V E L O P E R X N A V L I S C I E R B
M L G H U J V I T I L L U S T R A T O R N T R V
B H W A R I Q D A S N G S X E O D M F K T S P P
L O L J I O I F G J I O M I E W P O T C E Y P G
S T Z F R T T E F Y E T D G H U E Q W P R L V R
A R S P S B E S U B K C N W T L L R A M O A F A
F R C I U T R R E N G I S E D R O I R E T N I P
P L T H H Y N M L V F R R K I F X C E B C A X H
H R I T P Y S R M F N P B M Y C A D E A E S T I
A U P G P Y Z F N C R I P K Q S S W N M P S E C
R H N K H C H I R O P R A C T O R I G O S E I D
M A R K E T I N G M A N A G E R G U I A N N L E
A A H U Z K A R Y N A I R A R B I L N P I I A S
C M O T I V A T I O N A L S P E A K E R D S N A
I J P Z J M N I T M C H E M I S T E Y O U R G N
S W S S M C Y U R E U R U E D E T B R C O B U N
T W R E U G L R R C N D P O T Y A U G E F A O E
V Y R A T I L I M S P D I P C C H Z U W C S J R
B A Z I A Y T I H R E G A N A M S E L A S S O S
O P T O M E T R I S T O Q N J N F J A Y O R C C
R U J S V H L B V W A M S H T R H F B R H Z H O
K M L A N D S C A P E R O S H F W P R G R I K B
```

Word List
NURSE
CHEMIST
SCIENTIST
LANDSCAPER
OPTOMETRIST
WEB DEVELOPER
GRAPHIC DESIGNER
SOFTWARE ENGINEER
MOTIVATIONAL SPEAKER

ARTIST
INVESTOR
LIBRARIAN
PHARMACIST
CHIROPRACTOR
FOOD INSPECTOR
FLIGHT ATTENDANT
INTERIOR DESIGNER

PAINTER
MILITARY
JOURNALIST
ILLUSTRATOR
SALES MANAGER
BUSINESS ANALYST
MARKETING MANAGER
COMPUTER PROGRAMMER

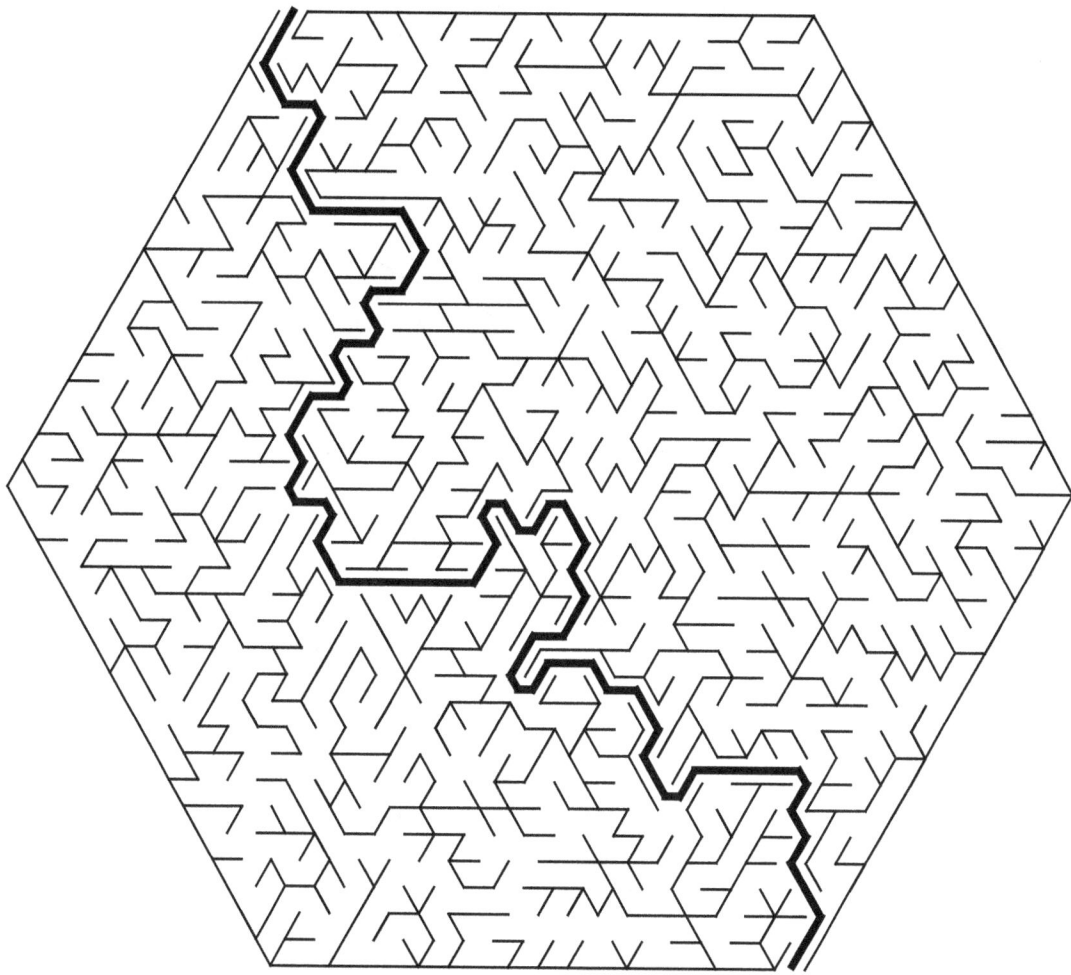
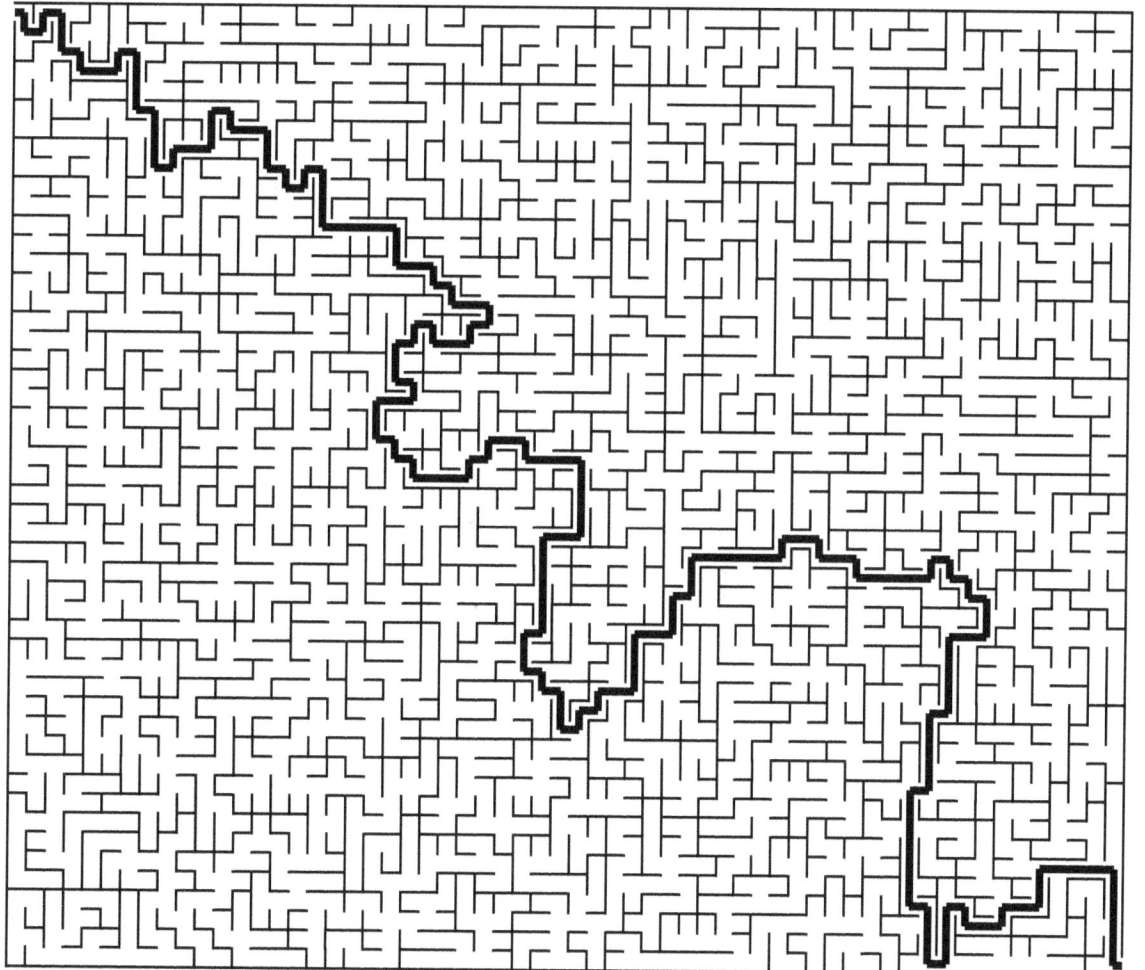

Click Here!
To see more Books
available by
Bri Jones

BriJonesMBA